EXPLORING YOUR ARTISTIC VOICE
IN CONTEMPORARY QUILT ART

SANDRA SIDER

SCHIFFER
PUBLISHING

4880 Lower Valley Road • Atglen, PA 19310

Other Books by the Author

Art Quilts Unfolding: 50 Years of Innovation, Sandra Sider, ed.; Nancy Bavor, Lisa Ellis, Martha Sielman, SAQA (Studio Art Quilt Associates, Inc.), ISBN 978-0-7643-5626-1

Other Schiffer Books on Related Subjects

Quilted Leather: Adding Texture, Dimension, and Style to Leather Crafting, Cathy Wiggins, ISBN 978-0-7643-5500-4

Art Quilts International: Abstract & Geometric, Martha Sielman, ISBN 978-0-7643-5220-1

Master Your Craft: Strategies for Designing, Making, and Selling Artisan Work, Tien Chiu, Foreword by Christopher H. Amundsen, Executive Director, American Craft Council, ISBN 978-0-7643-5145-7

Designed by Ashley Millhouse
Type set in AGaramond LT Titling/Agenda

Photos by the author unless otherwise noted.

ISBN: 978-0-7643-5887-6
Printed in China

Published by Schiffer Publishing, Ltd.
4880 Lower Valley Road
Atglen, PA 19310
Phone: (610) 593-1777; Fax: (610) 593-2002
E-mail: Info@schifferbooks.com
Web: www.schifferbooks.com

For our complete selection of fine books on this and related subjects, please visit our website at www.schifferbooks.com. You may also write for a free catalog.

Schiffer Publishing's titles are available at special discounts for bulk purchases for sales promotions or premiums. Special editions, including personalized covers, corporate imprints, and excerpts, can be created in large quantities for special needs. For more information, contact the publisher.

We are always looking for people to write books on new and related subjects. If you have an idea for a book, please contact us at proposals@schifferbooks.com.

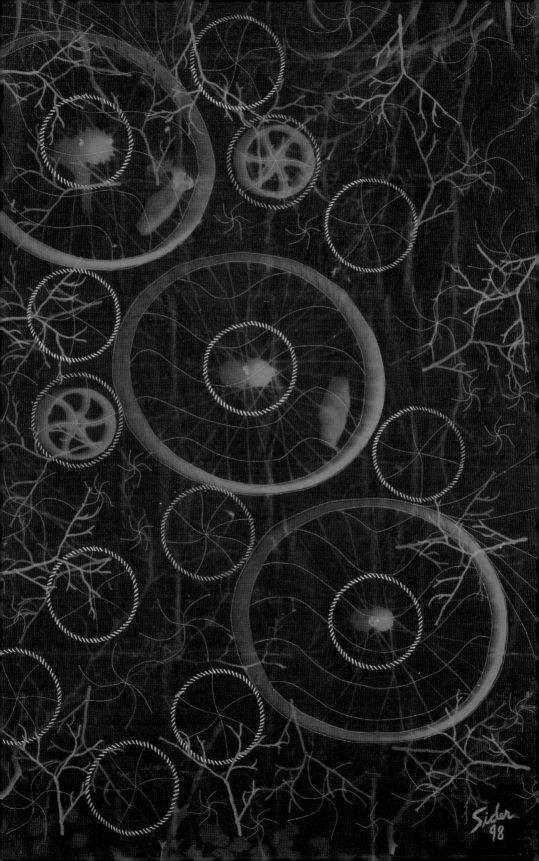

CONTENTS

INTRODUCTION

Think of the artists whose work you admire, individuals with a distinctive style or perhaps several styles developed over the years. You might like their use of color, materials, craft expertise, subject matter, wit, etc. But above all, you recognize in these makers an authenticity, a confident approach to the quilt medium. That is their artistic voice.

I decided to create a book about exploring one's artistic voice in response to the many questions I have had on this topic during two decades of leading art quilt critique workshops. Often the participants ask, "How do I develop my artistic voice, and what exactly is that?" This is the second most pervasive inquiry in the workshops, after "What happens to my quilts when I die?" I can't help artists with that one, but I have some advice from my personal perspective that blind alleys, detours, and the road not taken can all lead to developing one's voice as a quilt artist—indeed, as any sort of creative maker.

In explaining how I have explored and continue to explore my own voice in contemporary quilt art, I hope to encourage and enlighten other artists. The decision to use images of my own quilts as examples stems from my aversion to making extremely negative comments in a public forum on the work of others. Doing this book is a bit scary for me, but I have been inspired to take the leap by the closing words in Michele Obama's 2018 book *Becoming*: "There's power in allowing yourself to be known and heard, in owning your unique story, in using your authentic voice." I hope that the power will be yours as you explore your own voice.

Above all, you recognize an authenticity, a confident approach to the quilt medium: that is artistic voice.

You might like to know a few things about my background before delving into the book proper. My quilting roots are in Appalachia, where my paternal grandmother and aunt were making functional bed-sized quilts that probably would be considered folk art (figs. 1–3).

Fig. 1. Judith Saunders Herren. Bowtie, late 1950s. Photo by Karen Bell.

Fig. 2. Judith Saunders Herren. *Pinwheel Four-Patch*, 1970s. Photo by Karen Bell.

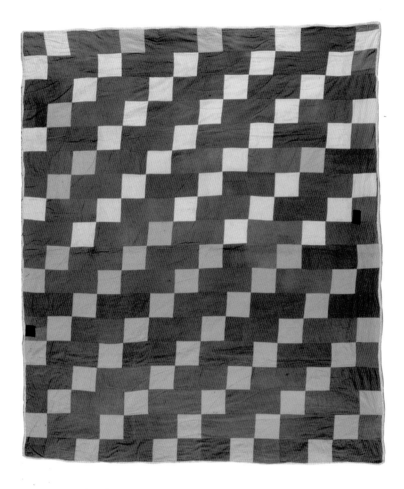

Fig. 3. Virginia Dare Saunders (my grandmother). *Streak of Lightning*, 1930s.
Photo by Karen Bell.

As a little girl, I would sit under the quilt being stitched on a frame by my female relatives, watching the light make multicolored patterns against the muslin backing fabric. Quilt making holds a mystique for me; I learned back then that sitting and working on something for hours not only is a valued way to spend time but also can seem to stop time. On many late afternoons, one of the quilters would be surprised to realize that suppertime was approaching. I would hear the question "Where in the world did the time go?" I wanted to experience that magic but did not understand it at the age of seven. I'm only beginning to understand it at the age of 70.

During the late 1970s in North Carolina, after my college years, I made traditional hand-stitched functional quilts for family and friends from all sorts of patterns—pieced, appliquéd, and embroidered (figs. 4–8). My hands were always busy, even embroidering quilt blocks for my daughter the day after she was born. After all, I had been taught the folk wisdom that "idle hands are the devil's workshop."

Fig. 4. *Domino Stripe* (variation of *Jacob's Ladder*, for my son Jacob), 1976. 68 × 48 in.

Fig. 5. *Abistar* (star quilt for my daughter Abigail), 1976. 65 × 52 in.

Fig. 6. *Moon over the Mountain*, 1976. 103 × 75 in. Private collection.

Fig. 8. *Coquelicot* ("Poppy"), 1977. 102 × 80 in. Private collection.

Fig. 7. *Semaphore for a Rainy Sunday*, 1983. 86 × 72 in. Private collection.

By the 1970s, there were several excellent books about making quilts. But I did not know that some of them were opening a new world of quilts as unique works of art. Then my husband and I lived for two years in Kentucky, where I saw several quilt exhibitions that included what I now realize were some amazing examples of Outsider Art that questioned my assumptions about quilts and their purposes.

We moved to New York City in 1979, where I began a new job in Manhattan. I found myself going to see photography exhibitions and became interested in contact printing—a one-to-one exact printing of an object or film image—and in different types of image transfer. For a few years, I abandoned quilts and thought that photography might satisfy my creative impulse. But I missed fondling fabric and smoothing it out as I folded it. The whir of my sewing machine also was conspicuously absent. If only I could sew my own images! I knew of industrial machines that printed commercial textiles and messy screen-printing techniques used by printmakers, but neither was practical in our small apartment and I could not afford to rent studio space.

Then I had one of those life-changing experiences that at the time might seem like nothing more than a fun day. An old friend from North Carolina, a photographer teacher, wanted to learn how to make a quilt. I knew the quilt-making half of that equation, and she knew the im-age-making half, teaching me about high-contrast negatives and cyanotype (blueprinting) chemicals. We spent hours mixing our chemicals and printing dozens of cotton rectangles with her cyanotype images on a sunny terrace in the Bronx. The deep Prussian blue of cyanotype percolated in my mind for more than ten years while I created photo transfer quilts in full color. But eventually cyanotype triumphed in my work, becoming my most authentic voice, and the story of how and why that happened composes the core of this book. I hope that my journey might give you some pointers for your own artistic path.

*Using your
authentic voice means
your work will
stand apart.*

HOW MANY THINGS
DO YOU KNOW?

Do you need to know anything at all beyond techniques, processes, and materials? Can we create meaningful art in a cultural void? Outsider artists drawing upon vivid imaginations function in their own private world, and I rather envy their complete independence from critics and curators. But assuming that you want others to see and appreciate your work, think about the fact that the word "voice" suggests having something to say. Your voice can be an advocate for beauty when you create a purely aesthetic quilt, or a persuasive piece using visual rhetoric. The trick is doing either or both with, in the words of philosopher Denis Dutton, "the complex expressive possibilities we observe in the great established art traditions of the world," while maintaining your own individual and unique character.

If making beautiful art quilts is your goal, you might want to study the historical continuum of the Art Quilt movement, discovering which artists appeal to you and analyzing their work. What sorts of fabrics do they use? How are their quilts structured? How do they incorporate embellishment? How does the stitching enhance their designs? It would also be helpful to familiarize yourself with the paintings, prints, and textile art of your own culture. How do those artists use texture, color, line, contrast, and mass—the basic principles of art? Do you notice any differences between how those makers apply the basic principles when compared with quilt artists? What I have noticed is that the latter prioritize the principle of texture. It's what we do. I find that a good art quilt should incorporate at least two of the basic principles of art (texture and one more), and at least two principles of design, among which are balance, unity, focal point, repetition of motif or color, and variation of scale.

During the late 1980s, my affinity for the grid format—which originally stemmed from traditional quilt making—was enriched by my personal discovery of Andy Warhol's silkscreen paintings using multiple images, especially his Marilyn Monroe pieces from the 1960s after her untimely death in 1962. Something about the color shifts in his grids of multiple images resonated with me, and in 1990 I made my first photo transfer quilt, a small piece with multiple images of cantaloupes (fig. 9).

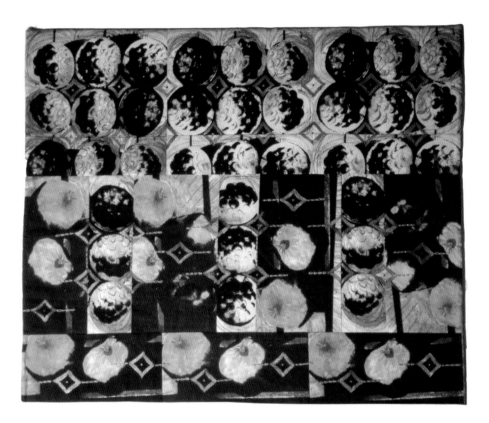

Fig. 9. *Cantaloupe Calliope*, 1990. 13 × 18 in.

I look at that quilt today and wonder what I thought I was trying to do. The quilt has no real content, and I can't remember why those embroidered orange diamonds were added, except that I felt a need to fill the murky black voids. The quilt is boring, a far cry from Warhol's charged surfaces dealing with celebrity and mortality. I did, however, learn two things from making this quilt: I'm not that fond of working in small format, and photographic imagery can be altered in interesting ways by drawing and coloring on clear plastic overlays. I would be using that technique for about ten years, until the effect could be easily achieved digitally. A better example of my early work with photo transfer using plastic overlays reproduces my photographs of a vintage lawn mower, with a proper focal point in the composition (fig. 10). I have a fondness for classic hand-operated machinery and tools, and that connection is obvious in the quilt.

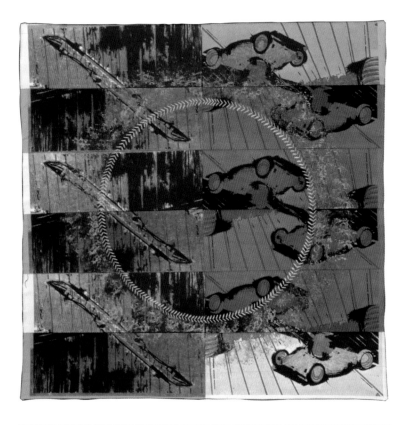

Fig. 10. *Mutant Mowers*, 1991. 22.5 × 22.5 in. Private collection.

*Steer away from a myopic attachment to
materials, techniques, or concepts.*

Creating an art quilt of timeless beauty requires a basic knowledge of color theory and composition, and of how our eyes perceive these aspects of quilt aesthetics. Beauty truly is in the eye of the beholder. We are not talking about "pretty" quilts here, but of abstract or representational artwork that expresses emotional depths of the artist, evoking similar responses in the viewer. The artwork does not have to be pleasing—it can even be sinister—as long as it speaks to the viewer in an authentic voice on a universal human level. To develop that level of emotional awareness as an artist, it would not hurt to familiarize yourself with some of the classic books of philosophy and literature. Aesthetics has a very wide lens, taking in all of human experience, while rhetoric has a much narrower focus, zooming in on a specific issue within a comparatively short time frame.

My artistic voice focuses more on communication than aesthetics, but earlier in my career I occasionally did not effectively communicate my contextual purpose because I was not considering broader aspects of my subjects. In critique workshops, I often mention how artists can have a myopic attachment to materials, techniques, or concepts. I know, because that has happened to me. My hope is to steer you away from some of the mistakes I have made as you strive for authenticity in your own work.

In the 1990s, for example, I was so enamored of photography that in one quilt I failed to consider the sexist overtones of an anticigarette piece (fig. 11). I intended to denigrate cigarette smoking, placing it in a seedy context, but succeeded only in denigrating the female figure. That was made clear to me by audience comments in a New York gallery when I exhibited the quilt. How I could have made this quilt in the midst of Anita Hill's testimony against Clarence Thomas as a Supreme Court nominee boggles my mind. I should have been more aware of third-wave feminism and its precepts.

Fig. 11. *Camel Chorus*, 1991. 34 × 24 in.

Consider color. It's important. In 1989, I was in Mexico City during the New Year's holiday, when there was some sort of threat near the British Embassy, with police in riot gear standing guard. I meant for the quilt concerning this experience to be ominous, reflecting the discomfort I felt walking back to my hotel in the dark. Looking at the quilt on display in an exhibition, it struck me that the cyanotype images printed on bubblegum-pink fabric lent a carnival air to the quilt, defeating my purpose (fig. 12). But I sure did like that pink cotton. My materials conflicted with my voice.

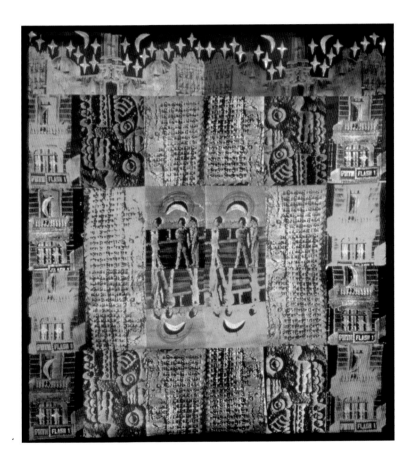

Fig. 12. *New Moon over Mexico*, 1990. 41 × 38 in. (unquilted top).

It seems to me that visual artists creating pieces for the wall have two main paths, either of which can successfully express your individual personality and voice. Both require foundational knowledge in different areas to create exciting work. If you want to make beautiful art quilts, then learn something about aesthetics and how beauty has been defined, and by whom. Let that information steep in your mind as you delve into your psyche to select colors and shapes for each new quilt. If you want to create quilts persuading your audience to a particular point of view, or simply open a dialogue about a specific issue, you need to inform yourself about all arguments, pro and con. That is not an easy task in today's world, bombarded as we are with conflicting opinions and fake "news" on all sides. Learn to read between the lines, considering your sources, to arrive at a plausible path to each new work. If you are lucky, you might bring both approaches together in the same quilt, resulting in a beautiful work of art rich with meaningful content.

*What will
your design say?
Know that message
and consider context.*

HOW MANY THINGS
CAN YOU DO?

I ask this question not so you can pat yourself on the back about how many studio workshops you have taken or how many processes and techniques you have studied. Let me rephrase the question: How many things can you do *well*? During the last decade of the 20th century I thought that I had to buy every book and magazine about putting imagery onto fabric—"surface design" was my constant search term.

Fig. 13. *Red River*, 1999. 35 × 35 in. (I learned at Quilt Surface Design Symposium that working with batik is not for me—the fumes made me sick—although I do like how this silk quilt catches the light). Photo by Karen Bell.

Fig. 14. *Pink Safari*, 1991. 19 × 23 in. (printing multiple images for no good reason, just because I could, and with a very dead focal point smack in the center). Private collection.

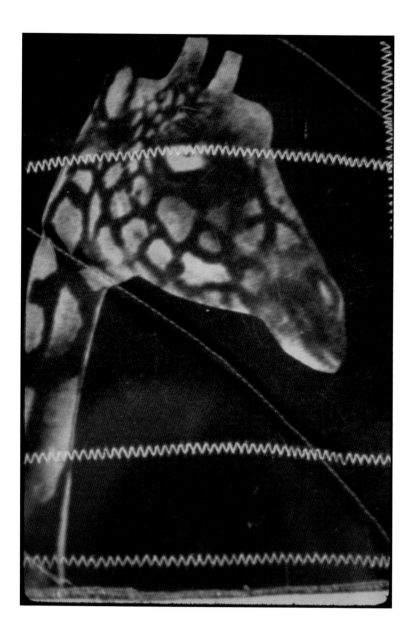

Fig. 15. Detail from *Ground Zero*, 1986 (printing negative images in cyanotype would become an important process a few years later, as in fig. 12). Private collection.

I took courses in silk painting, silk screening, intaglio printing, Polaroid transfer, cyanotype, dyeing, batik, and more. Recognizing that the results of my work in some of these processes were acceptable but not great, I felt that I was on the right track but riding the wrong train. But my time was not wasted because I was learning about approaches that did not inspire my voice and some that did (figs. 13–15). Of all those processes, today cyanotype figures large in my artistic toolbox. I am now confident in how much I can do with cyanotype, but it took three decades to arrive at this point (figs. 16–20).

Fig. 19. *Penumbra #7: Twilight*, 2007. 41 × 29 in. Photo by Deidre Adams.

Fig. 16. *Eyes of Egypt*, 1989. 39 × 36 in. (unquilted top).

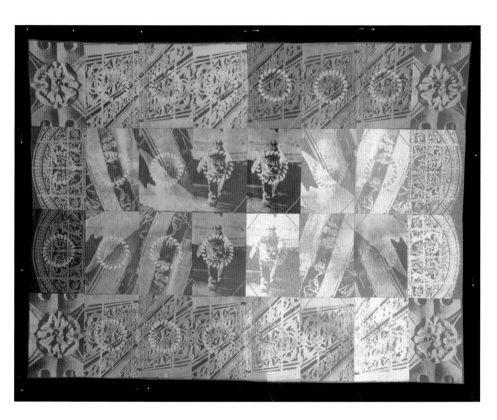

Fig. 17. *Chapultepec Flash*, 1990. 37 × 50 in. (unquilted top).

Fig. 18. *Stir Crazy*, 2002. 60 × 42 in. Photo by Karen Bell. Collection of the
International Quilt Museum, University of Nebraska.

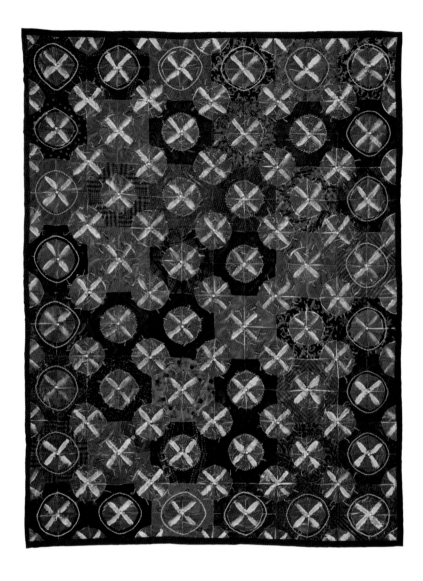

Fig. 20. *Past Present: Snowball Effect*, 2016. 59 × 44.5 in. Photo by Deidre Adams.

Doing something well builds confidence, and I have found that doing just about *anything* well builds confidence. Sometimes a quilt artist will ask me, "How do I know when I should feel proud of my work, when I have accomplished what I set out to do when making a quilt?" My response to that sort of insecurity is this: "What are the significant accomplishments in your life—not your career, but in general?" We all have areas of excellence, reasons to feel a sense of pride. Do you enjoy cooking a fancy meal? Are you a talented gardener? Are you a whiz with number puzzles? An excellent swimmer? A civic organizer? Think of the feeling you have after accomplishing a demanding task. You see, you already know what confidence feels like, so allow yourself to discover some element of your completed quilt that gives you that same feeling. Whether it's the color, composition, texture, size, or concept, the part of your work that speaks to you, that makes you proud, is hinting at your artistic voice.

You know what confidence feels like.
Pinpoint its sources in your work.

What makes you happy when you are working on a new piece? For me, I realized long ago that printing in cyanotype, which deeply saturates any natural fiber, makes me happy.

Fig. 21. *Twilight Forest*, 2018. 20 × 30 in. Cyanotype photograms of foliage sun-printed on paper. Private collection (commissioned, in collaboration with KOM Studio).

Fig. 22. *Going Home*, 2002. 70 × 52 in. Photo by Karen Bell.

That rich blue printed on paper can be satisfying, but printing on fabric gives the imagery many possibilities (figs. 21–22). This is the gist of why I make art quilts instead of prints on paper. Have you figured out why *you* work with quilts as an art form, as opposed to or in addition to other mediums? What specific steps do you look forward to the most when beginning a new quilt?

The choices you've made can be clues to developing your voice.

Your degree of excitement and involvement with the quilt-making experience can indicate avenues to explore (or not) as you develop your artistic voice. What do you do as you approach a new project? If you find yourself dallying and postponing the first steps of creating a new quilt, then you probably are heading in the wrong direction. If you find yourself checking your phone and surfing the internet instead of getting to work on that quilt, then you definitely need to reconsider what you were planning to do. Avoiding a new project can be your inner voice helping you change direction.

Fig. 23. *Boogie-Down Kitchen*, 2000. 40 × 35 in. Cyanotype photograms of kitchen tools, a chair, and large pulley wheels found in a salvage shop. Photo by Karen Bell.

Fig. 24. *Water Wheels*, 1998. 62 × 43 in. Cyanotype photograms of tree branches, bicycle wheels, and small pulley wheels found in a salvage shop. Photo by Karen Bell. Collection of Atlanta International Airport (Concourse C).

Your artistic voice is a process . . .
one that doesn't end.

"Artistic voice" is sometimes described as a goal to achieve, as if we finally get to ring that bell once we find it. But I think of artistic voice as an ongoing process—thus the word "exploring" in this book's title rather than "finding." The touchstone for my artistic voice is photographic imagery, transforming seemingly mundane aspects of our lives into something new and exciting (figs. 23–24). But sometimes I become so entranced by the process of creating the imagery that I lose sight of my ultimate goal of making an appealing art quilt. Even when that sidetracking has happened, I still completed the quilt, honing my craft skills in the process while thinking about how I went wrong (fig. 25).

Fig. 25. *Step Right Up!*, 1999. 53 × 40 in. (I got a bit carried away with stamping in purple paint with the sole of my boot, partially obscuring the photo-transferred imagery). Photo by Karen Bell.

Fig. 26. *Garden Grid #1*, 2011. 37 × 39 in. (Do let me know if *you* can see any reason for that purple netting.) Photo by Deidre Adams.

Whatever gives you a thrill in your creative process can be a double-edged sword. On the one hand, machine quilting can get out of hand and dominate the surface, messages can become strident rather than persuasive, colors can become overwhelming, and too much embellishment can obscure your purpose, just to give a few examples (fig. 26). On the other hand, any or all of these aspects of an art quilt could signify your distinctive voice, once you have achieved a unified surface that is yours and yours alone (figs. 27–28).

Fig. 27. *Garden Grid #2*, 2011. 40 × 38 in. Photo by Deidre Adams.

Next page: Fig. 28. Detail of *Garden Grid #2*, 2011. Sunflowers stamp-printed in metallic gold with a potato masher (and I was loving how that paint clings to the edges of the stamped lines). Photo by Deidre Adams.

Some lucky souls seem to be born with a sense of design, but most of us have to work on training our eyes. Until you have a chance to explore the possibilities of art and design, and to learn the skills needed to apply yourself in your chosen art form, you won't be able to sense your artistic voice as it develops. Art classes in general and studio workshops in particular give you the ability to audition various approaches to composition.

You might begin your art quilt journey by imitating the work of your teachers, getting a feel for whether you like dealing with commercial fabrics or prefer to jump into dyes and other types of surface design. Only by doing can you discover what seems most natural to you, what techniques and processes complement your personal vision and express your ideas most completely. Only by doing can you determine whether your work space or your physical limitations preclude an art activity, or that you can conquer those problems with specialized tools or by reorganizing your space. You need to feel comfortable in your studio, letting yourself become attuned to what feels most natural as you create your quilts. Listen to your inner voice, the magical power that can make time seem to stand still when you are in the zone. That zone is where your artistic voice will flourish.

*To become attuned to
your voice, work to
understand what
you already do and
already know.*

DOES YOUR ART
EDUCATION EVER END?

Raise your hand if you have taken a lot of art, craft, or quilting classes. My hand is certainly up. I think of all the classes I have taken to discover the perfect combination of techniques and processes to fulfill my own voice. Unlike scientific research, which has a disinterested goal of understanding basic truths of nature, artistic research is purely personal, an idiosyncratic quest to explore our expressive possibilities. There is no basic truth about art making because the very definition of art can change within its cultural setting, and even within an individual artist as that person matures and evolves.

You may find that studying one technique can lead to another as your voice develops. After learning how to screen print on fabric, I wanted to personalize and enhance the imagery with hand printing. That need took me to a book on stamp printing, and I found myself cutting designs into erasers, as well as heading out to antique shops to look for old tools such as timbale rosettes and odd-shaped potato mashers. That one screen-printing course opened a door that has not yet closed. I began painting, stamp printing, and sponge printing on cyanotype images and photo transfers in addition to my screen-printed textiles. Be open to such impulses, because they might surprise you (figs. 29–31).

As your voice becomes distinct,
a technique may lead to valuable
new impulses and clarity.

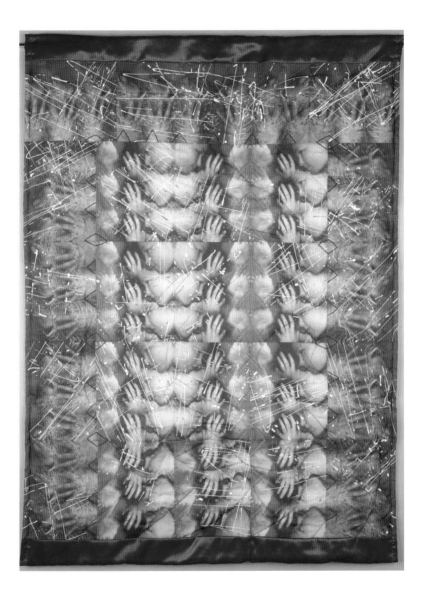

Fig. 29. *Women at Work and Play #2*, 1992. 50 × 36 in. Portraits of the artist taken by KOM Studio with a Polaroid camera, slash painted by pumping a syringe. Photo by the artist.

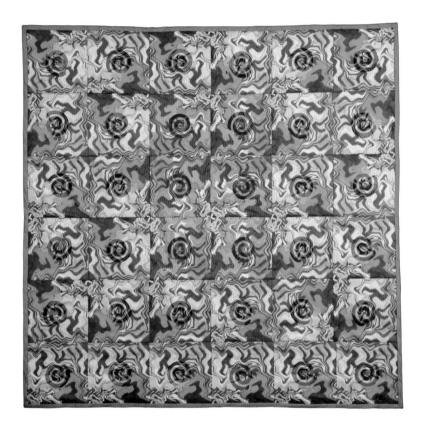

Fig. 30. *On the Road: Road Rage*, 2010. 40 × 41 in. Artist's digital image of a license plate manipulated with the "liquefy" tool and photo transferred, stamp printed with spiral motfis. Photo by Deidre Adams.

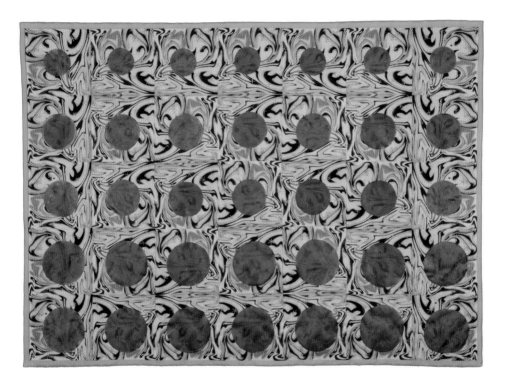

Fig. 31. *On the Road, High Water*, 2010. 31 × 42 in. Artist's digital image of a license plate manipulated with the "liquefy" tool and photo transferred, circles painted with a brush. Photo by Deidre Adams.

Going to museum and gallery exhibitions should be part of your continuing art education as you explore your voice throughout your career. Quilt exhibitions, of course, should be on your list—quilts of all styles and all eras. Several contemporary quilt artists of note found their color palette or graphic impetus in antique Amish quilts. You never know when inspiration might strike. Consider expanding your horizon by viewing exhibitions of other mediums, especially paintings, photographs, and prints to study composition and color. Even sculptural works could speak to you through mass and form. While images of artwork in books can pique your interest, there is no substitute for studying original art. Color saturation, texture, scale, and other aspects are usually lost in books, and they are most definitely lost in online images.

When viewing art by others, you are not comparing your work to theirs, but instead opening yourself to discover artwork that activates your voice and sends you back to the studio in a state of excitement. Instead of saying, "Oh, I could never make something so amazing," think about how that amazing piece can spark your own creativity. It could be nothing more than your realization that a certain shade of purple next to a certain shade of green lights up something in your brain, or that metallic fabric could enhance your next quilt. Remember that you are creating art in your own unique space and time. You are not Georgia O'Keeffe, but then she could never be *you*.

If you are invited to teach an art quilt workshop, consider taking advantage of that opportunity. Through the years, I have found that teaching has helped develop my artistic voice as much as anything else. Students in critique workshops as well as studio classes are curious about what their teachers are doing. Verbalizing how and especially why you create art quilts can help focus your voice.

Occasionally you might be rewarded for teaching with a bonus, a gifted student who teaches you something new or responds to your artwork in a new way. Seeing your own work through different eyes can send you in an exciting new direction.

Fig. 32. *Women at Work and Play #1*, 1992. 54 × 39 in. Private collection.

Fig. 33. *Women at Work and Play #4*, 1993. 47 × 47 in.

Does your voice resonate with history, politics, nature, science? The more informed you are about areas of interest, the more complex your quilts will be. I find that creating visual art is the opposite process of writing (the right-brain/left-brain dichotomy), but that reading enriches both endeavors. I recently listed my ten favorite books and why they made the list. To my surprise, a theme of strong, confident female characters ran through most of them, suggesting that a significant aspect of my artistic voice has been developing since I was a teenager (*Jane Eyre*). One of my projects from the 1990s reflects that feminist theme, which obviously is important to me (figs. 29 and 32–33). Try listing your own ten favorite books, to get to know yourself better. Unless you know yourself, you cannot possibly know what you want to say in your art quilts.

You are not Georgia O'Keeffe, but then she could never be you.

Knowing what resonates with you and your personal experiences can lead to stimulating art quilts. The two quilts in figures 30 and 31, along with six others, resulted from a solo cross-country drive that I did in 2008, photographing distinctive license plates along the way. The quilt titles reflect various road signage, with one special quilt incorporating images of several license plates, since *Curves Ahead* became a metaphor for all the snags I encountered during the trip (figs. 34–35).

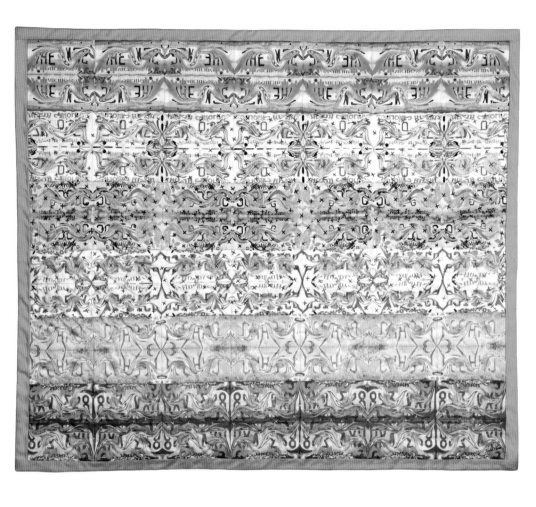

Fig. 34. *On the Road: Curves Ahead*, 2010. 35 × 41 in. Photo by Deidre Adams.

Fig. 35. Detail of *On the Road: Curves Ahead*, 2010. Photo by Deidre Adams.

Besides studies pertaining to your art making, you need to learn a few things about the business of being a visual artist, some of which is covered in the final chapter of this book. But here let's address learning to create your portfolio, the most crucial component of publicizing your art career. A lot has been written about creating a "body of work" and what that means. It does not mean making a dozen quilts in the same series or in the same style and grouping them in your website or brochure.

You will be selecting the quilts in which you have mastered techniques and processes, and that best communicate your artistic vision. They also should show a chronological range of your work, indicating the breadth of your career. Above all else, the quality of your content will make or break your portfolio, and that means not only your quilt images but also additional information—cover letter, brief biography, resume, and checklist of images. Whether submitting your portfolio (digital or actual) to an art school, gallery, museum, or potential client, present your work as a coherent unit, with all the quilts photographed against a similar neutral background and preferably by the same photographer. You want your unique voice to come through clear and strong, without any fussy distractions.

Throughout your career, learning never ends, a fact well recognized by some of the greatest artists. In one of his last letters, Paul Cézanne at an advanced age expressed a desire to "continue his studies." That is a pretty good example to follow.

*Seek out learning
opportunities to
intensify your
voice's richness.*

YOU CALL YOURSELF
AN ARTIST

Until you truly think of yourself as an artist, it would be futile to attempt to explore and develop your artistic voice. What is your "elevator pitch" when a stranger asks you what you do? Here is my answer: "I'm an artist. I work mostly with photographic imagery in textiles—art quilts. And I write about contemporary art as well as curating exhibitions." Then the stranger gets a big, warm smile from me, indicating that I am proud and happy with what I just said. Notice that I lead with "artist," not "quilts," then bring quilts into the conversation. Because of preconceived notions concerning quilt culture, you could lose your audience at "quilt" if you began by saying "quilt artist." I used to lead with "I'm a quilt artist," at which, more times than not, the person with whom I was speaking at a non-quilt gallery opening or other event would glance beyond me and say something like "Oh, excuse me, I see someone I know."

I have observed so many artists, especially women and especially quilt artists, seeming to apologize about what they do. They hem and haw, shuffle their feet, play with their hair, look sideways, and speak in a hesitant manner. If you do not believe in yourself as an artist, neither will anyone else. Whether an amateur or professional (i.e., making money from your art), if you are making art, then you are an artist. The art does not even have to be good. Weekend painters are artists, even though they paint for themselves and have regular jobs during the week. While I have sold some of my quilts and made some commissioned work, most of my quilts are created because I am compelled by my nature to work in the studio. That satisfies a basic urge.

You may have heard a lot about "branding" yourself as an artist, but that would mean that you use your voice to create a single, focused, consistent style appealing to a specific audience or market. I view that process as industrializing art. Through half a century of quilt making, my own work has changed dramatically (figs. 36–40).

Fig. 36. *Heliotrope*, 1984. 38 × 55 in.

Fig. 37. *Knight Watch*, 1991. 40 × 31 in. Private collection.

Fig. 38. *Text and Commentary*, 2002. 22 × 25 in.

Fig. 39. *Garden Grid #4*, 2012. 28.5 × 43 in. Photo by Deidre Adams.

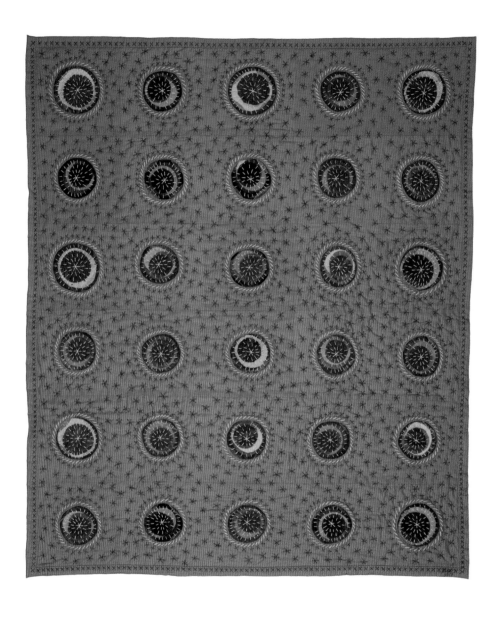

Fig. 40. *Past Present: Oculi*, 2017. 47 × 39 in. Photo by Deidre Adams.

The demands of daily life can feed your artistic voice.

The only common denominator, the foundation of my artistic voice, consists of photographic imagery. My work says, "Look here—see this! It means something to me and, I hope, to you." Artists actually should expect their voices to change and develop over the course of their careers, conditioned by their experiences. Often, I hear quilt artists express regret about how the events and demands of their daily lives impinge on their creative time, but those experiences can feed your artistic voice. My quilts, for example, took a turn toward environmental activism after my grandchildren were born. I considered their futures and my worldview expanded, to the point that today I am working on an entire cyanotype series about marine ecosystems (figs. 41–44).

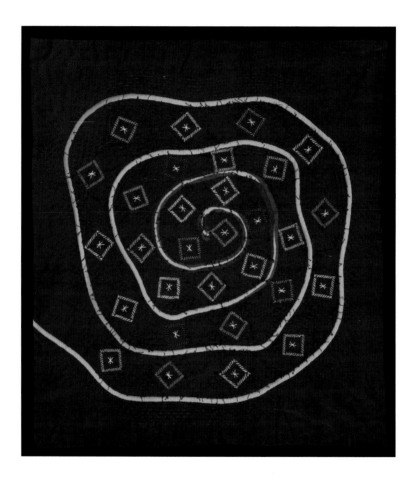

Fig. 41. *Tunicata I: Flotsam and Jetsam*, 2018. 40 × 36 in. Photo by Deidre Adams.

Fig. 42. *Tunicata II: Spin Control*, 2018. 39.5 × 35 in. Photo by Deidre Adams.

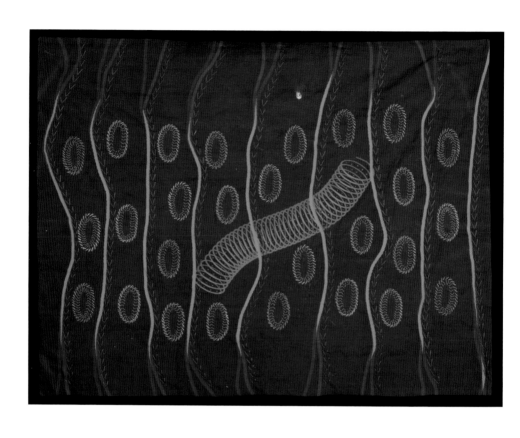

Fig. 43. *Tunicata III: Grassroots*, 2019. 30 × 39.5 in. Photo by Deidre Adams.

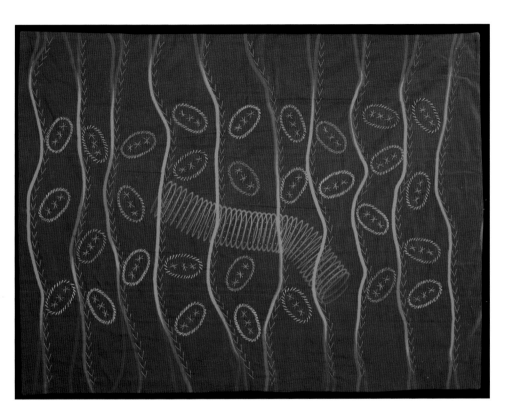

Fig. 44. *Tunicata IV: Grass Party*, 2019. 30 × 39.5 in. Photo by Deidre Adams.

The important thing is always to be aware of what your voice is trying to say, and you cannot explore your own voice when bombarded by all the digital noise of today's world. Your brain is always busy, and you need to pay attention to it. Even on your busiest days, try to set aside just ten minutes of quiet solitude and sift through creative impulses that may be percolating. Have a notepad handy to jot down ideas—an actual pad of paper, not a digital device, because then you might start checking email and texts. You may be surprised at the ideas that bubble up. This very private process is the opposite of spiritual mindfulness, being totally aware in the present moment. While that meditative activity can be beneficial to your state of mind, you also should practice internal mindfulness, being aware of what your mind, powered by your amazing brain, can tell you. Some people call it inspiration.

Your artistic voice originates in you, and you can work to develop it. Your voice depends on your unique personality, perceptions, and preferences. While you cannot always be completely independent in your studio work—for example, when creating a quilt for a competition with a specific theme or required format—you should have a feel for what materials, techniques, and processes resonate with your particular expertise and interests. By following your idiosyncratic tendencies, you have an excellent chance of developing a distinctive, original voice in your artwork.

Finally, when talking about where our artistic voices lead us, let's use "quilt artist" instead of "art quilter," which I avoid, as well as "art quilting." In no other field of art does a person say "art" followed by a noun of action. Think about it. The format typically follows a pattern of stating the material or process plus the noun of action—metal sculptor, watercolor artist, tapestry artist, printmaker. If we conform to the critical norms of the art world, then "quilt artists" have a better chance of being taken seriously. In addition, quilting is sometimes secondary in our art-work, which features numerous other techniques and processes. We are quilt artists when we bring all that together in the quilt medium, and saying "art quilter" focuses too heavily on the quilting. Your voice has a wider reach.

*Be deliberately
aware of your voice to
distinguish it from the
noise all around you.*

WHY CRITIQUES CAN
BE HELPFUL

Feel free to skip this chapter if you are completely confident in everything you make and have never asked yourself "What now?" in the midst of a project, becoming unsure about how to proceed. Have you ever wanted to ask another artist to study your work in progress and weigh in on how it seems to be proceeding? We all can appreciate the intentions of a loved one who says, "That's really nice!" But how helpful is that opinion when you yourself know that something has gone amiss and your concept is not being fully realized?

In this chapter, I am going to critique two of my early art quilts to demonstrate how a more critical eye could have helped me express my voice. During the early 1990s, I was making quilts without the support of a community of artists because I was unaware that any existed. Of course, this was prior to the explosion of internet communication, when all we had were print publications covering art and craft.

Critical input enables you to fully realize your design concept.

Today my critique workshops function very differently from what you will read below. In the workshops, I function more as a moderator than as an authority, with everyone encouraged to offer suggestions and comments. We begin by the artist explaining her/his concept for the quilt and whether any aspects of working on the piece have presented a challenge or problem. Then I make a few suggestions, after which the audience participates. The purpose of the workshop, which always has a friendly atmosphere, is to help the artist take that quilt down the road on which it is already heading—not to usurp the artist's intention. But in this chapter, I am going to be scathingly honest about what is lacking in my pieces, to give you an idea of the potential benefits of having your artwork critiqued by someone with an experienced eye.

Fig. 45. *The Woodlawn Waltz*, 1990. 32 × 35 in.

The Woodlawn Waltz (1990), one of my earliest cyanotype quilts, is printed with negative images because I like that eerie effect (fig. 45). I took the photographs in New York's Woodlawn Cemetery, and the images are hand stitched with outlines of coffins. At this time, I was structuring my cyanotype quilts by pillowcasing and tacking the top to a canvas back because I wanted them to look more like prints than quilts. That was my worst mistake. When I exhibited a selection of these quilts in a 1993 solo exhibition at Sarah Lawrence College, I noticed that areas of the surfaces were slightly sagging. The idea of a hybrid format between prints and quilt resulted in a technical failure. Regardless of the aesthetics or content of our quilts, we need to begin by recognizing that we *are* making quilts, with the requisite structural support.

My voice was not clear, so neither was my artwork.

Now let's look at the composition, with regard to the five basic principles of art—texture, color, line, contrast, and mass—as well as several principles of design, which, as you may recall, include balance, unity, focal point, movement, repetition, and scale. *The Woodlawn Waltz* has plenty of contrast and texture, both physical and visual, also a pleasing balance of warm and cool hues, but too much movement, without any sort of focal point where your eye can rest. The design is unbalanced, with statues aligned across the top and a narrow vista at the bottom. It would have been better if those two elements had been switched, opening the composition up at the top. And replacing the top four rectangles in the center with an inscription from a tombstone could have created a focal point. The quilt's subject is Woodlawn Cemetery, and I meant for the theme to be mortality. But my voice was not clear, and neither is my artwork.

Fig. 46. *Joystick*, 1991. 40 × 44 in.

Joystick (1991) is an early photo transfer quilt, also pillowcased and tacked to a canvas back (fig. 46). You would never guess that the subject of this piece is a Bell helicopter, an example of modern design, suspended from the ceiling of the Museum of Modern Art in New York. I love how that heavy piece of machinery seems light as air, hovering beside the walkway. As you can see, I had discovered fabric markers and went a little bit out of control. My intention was to mimic the actions of a gaming joystick, but the result looks like doodling. The dark, massive central area with lighter spots in the background certainly creates a sense of depth, but that dark imagery is turgid and confusing, and I made it worse by adding texture with blue paint. And why all the pink? When I saw this quilt reproduced in black and white, the design was still too busy, but the absence of color was a relief. That really told me something. From the beginning of work on this quilt, my favorite part was the row of four multiple images of the helicopter's transparent bubble canopy. I intended to celebrate the buoyant feeling of flight, but I was sidetracked. This quilt could have succeeded had I simply reproduced that image in several rows, subtly manipulating color values for variety and balance.

The lesson here is that each artwork needs clarity of purpose, even if you begin by just playing with fabrics, dyes, tools, etc. Think about whether you want the quilt to be a beautiful object (the aesthetic approach) or communicate a message (the rhetorical approach). If you run into problems or are unsure of where the quilt is going, don't hesitate to reach out to the art quilt community for advice. Sometimes the help is nothing more than information about a better tool or process. But sometimes it can change everything.

Your purpose for the
art must be clear.
Input can make all the
difference in freeing
your voice.

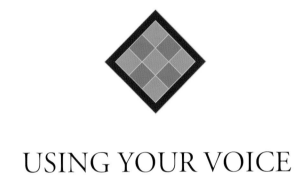

USING YOUR VOICE

Once you feel secure in the direction you are going with art quilts, your voice needs to flourish as you explore your style. The two best ways to do that are to make sure that you have the necessary skills for what you want to accomplish, and to create adequate space in which to work and to store your materials and tools. Many artists advocate a well-lit, windowless studio to avoid distractions from the exterior. That works for me—I keep the curtains closed over my studio windows except when using a process requiring ventilation. If possible, set aside a room exclusively for your art making. If instead you have to work in an area of a larger room, set up a folding screen or hang a large curtain that you can use to indicate "do not disturb," unless you live alone. Your studio time is "me time," and you should respect and protect it. If necessary, invest in a set of noise-dampening earphones. Mine have saved my sanity numerous times in the midst of what seems like endless street repairs and construction in my Bronx neighborhood.

Whether on social media or on paper, you need to describe what you've created, and describe it well.

Let's assume that you have reached a point where you know what you want to say with your art quilts and you know how to do it. If you have not done so already, do some research to locate a critique group or similar networking possibilities among local artists. They do not necessarily have to be quilt artists, but they should be visual artists serious about their work. Joining an art group could present opportunities for exhibiting and selling your work regionally. I have discovered through interviews with gallery owners that most customers prefer to purchase art by local and regional artists, and sometimes those purchases lead to additional pieces being purchased directly from the artists, and to commissioned work.

You need to be publicizing yourself, and social media can be effective if you are careful not to let it consume too much of your time. In spite of our digital age, people still like to have business cards and postcards from artists whose work interests them. Select your very best quilt for the postcard image and have it professionally photographed. One thing to remember: Many older people beset with vision problems collect art and have the money to buy it. Make it easy for them to read whatever is written on your business card, postcards, and website. Avoid smaller fonts and gray-on-gray design. You want as many people as possible attracted to your website to experience your unique artwork.

Just as you have worked toward developing your artistic voice, you need to have a distinctive voice to describe and discuss your work. Quilt artists usually are asked to make an "artist's statement" for each piece whenever they enter competitions and in exhibitions for which catalogs are created. I have read some truly awful statements in my career as a juror and curator, as well as statements nicely describing the artist but revealing nothing about the quilt. Here are a few examples of an artist's statements, using my own work as illustrations with both bad and good descriptions.

Penumbra #8: Love Letters

No: I found some lovers' graffiti carved into cactus leaves in Mexico City, and thought that the letters made an interesting pattern.

Yes: Lovers' names carved into cactus leaves were distorted and partially erased as the cactus grew into an aging plant. Here their names are memorialized in time, locked into a spiral.

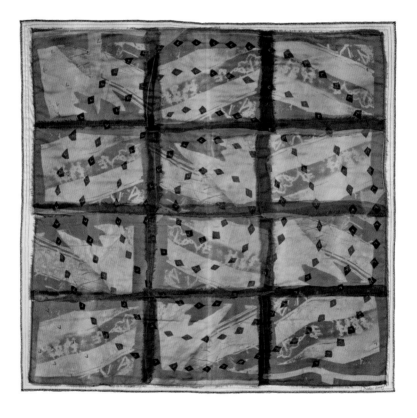

Fig. 45. *Penumbra #8: Love Letters*, 2007. 35 × 35 in. Photo by Deidre Adams.

Garden Grid #4

No: Weaving the strips together took many hours of careful work. But I am happy with my garden scene.

Yes: This series is inspired by aerial photographs of ancient garden grids in the Southwest, sustainable plots laid out in grids by Native Americans, which required minimal irrigation.

Fig. 46. *Garden Grid #3*, 2011. 36.5 × 39 in. Photo by Deidre Adams.

Past Present: Out of the Blue

No: I am celebrating Gershwin's "Rhapsody in Blue" with rope swirls and jazzy patterns using cyanotype.

Yes: "Out of the Blue" refers to the process used here, Prussian blue cyanotype, with serendipitous patterns resulting from cotton blends resisting the photographic chemicals. Using rope, I drew my interpretation of swooping, expansive music in Gershwin's "Rhapsody in Blue." My Past Present series incorporates traditional vintage quilt blocks and tops assembled by anonymous makers, creating contemporary statements.

Fig. 47. *Past Present: Out of the Blue*, 2018. 35 × 51.5 in. Photo by Deidre Adams.

Swept into Eternity

No: I think that the Trail of Tears was a horrible event in American history. It was said that the Cherokee were "swept into eternity." The footprints here represent people walking.

Yes: As members of the Cherokee nation were forced by the US government to walk the hellish Trail of Tears in the 1830s, from their lands in the East to Oklahoma, many hundreds died along the way, including children. In the words of Lucy Ames Butler, a Presbyterian missionary and wife of a minister who supported the Cherokee and traveled with them, these souls were "swept into Eternity by the cupidity of the white man who is in the enjoyment of wealth and freedom on the original soil of these oppressed Indians."

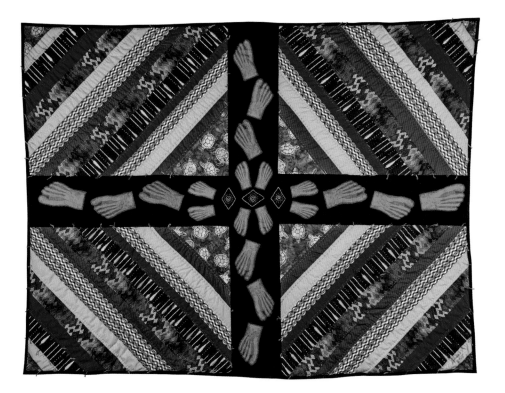

Fig. 48. *Swept into Eternity*, 2015. 56 × 75.5 in. Photo by Deidre Adams. Collection of the Newark Museum.

You get the picture, so to speak. There is no need to belabor the obvious, and beginning your statement with "I" diverts attention from the quilt, resulting in a weak artist's statement. Each statement about your quilt should briefly explain why you made it—why you felt compelled by your voice to complete that particular work of art.

As you explore your unique artistic voice, your work will mature and you will find yourself becoming more confident and perhaps even happy with what you are doing in the studio. That is my wish for you and why I wrote this book.

Respecting your voice means stronger work, confidence, and more fulfillment.

GALLERY

Cyanotype Quilt Images

Illustrating the Diversity of the Cyanotype Process

All photographs by Deidre Adams

Fig. 49. *Penumbra #2: Silent Soldiers*, 2007. 34.5 × 35 in.

Fig. 50. *Penumbra #3: Rule of Silence*, 2007. 35 × 35.5 in.

Fig. 51. *Penumbra #4: Reliquary*, 2007. 35 × 35 in.

Fig. 52. *Penumbra #6: Afternoon*, 2007. 41 × 29 in.

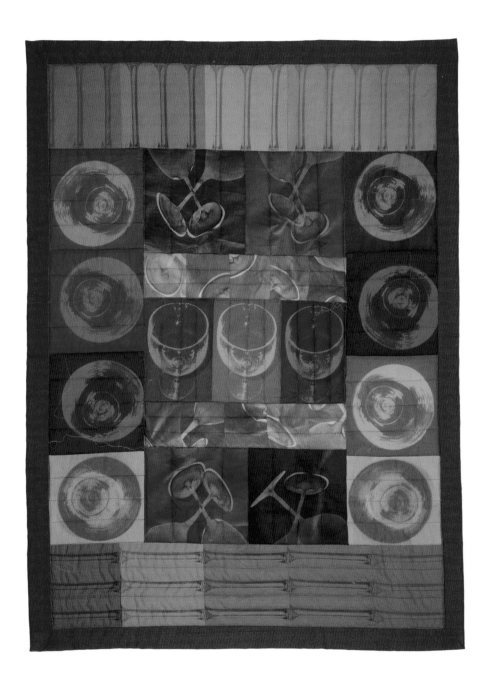

Fig. 53. *Bottoms Up!*, 2013. 44 × 32 in.

Fig. 54. *White Noise*, 2014. 28 × 32 in.

Fig. 55. *Sashay*, 2016. 27.5 × 28.5 in.

Fig. 56. *Stem Cells*, 2016. 46 × 39.5 in. Collection of Visions Art Museum, San Diego.

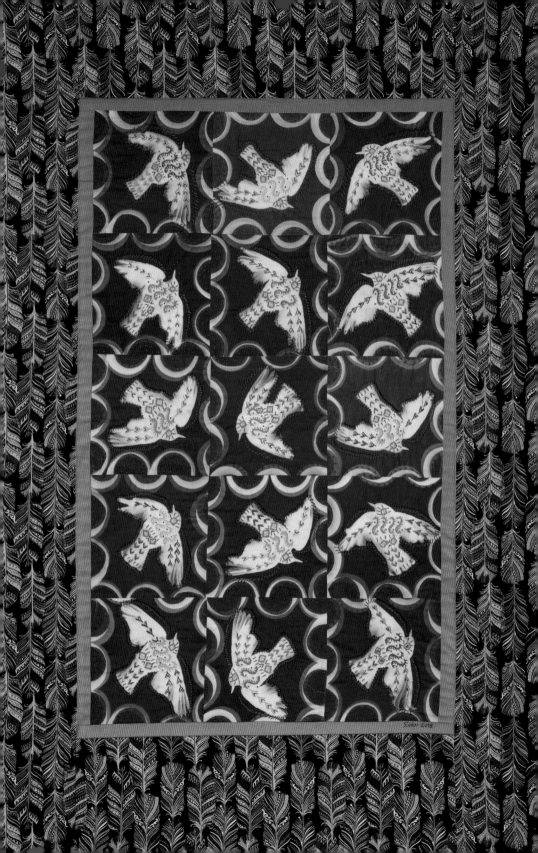

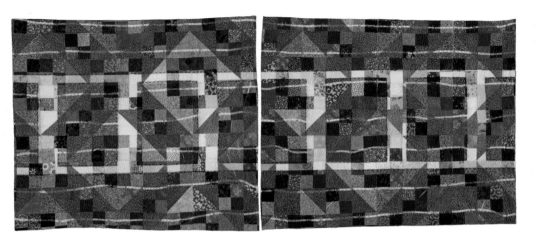

Fig. 58. *Past Present: Checkpoint*, 2018. 30 × 72.5 overall (diptych).

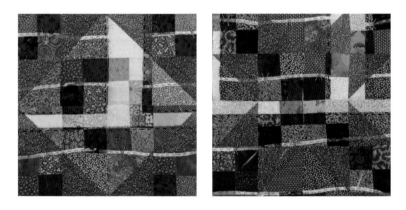

Details, Fig. 58.

Left: Fig. 57. *A Clear and Present Danger*, 2018. 54 × 38 in.

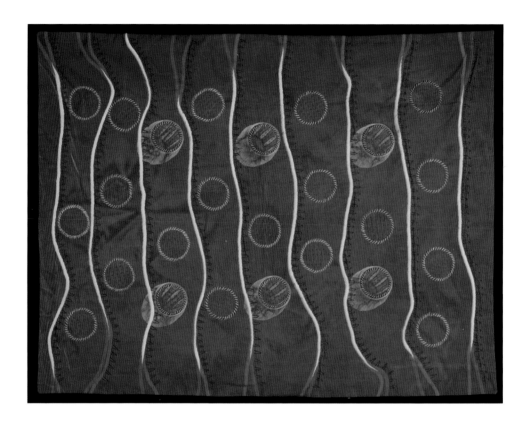

Fig. 59. *Tunicata V: Staying Afloat*, 2019. 30 × 39.5 in.

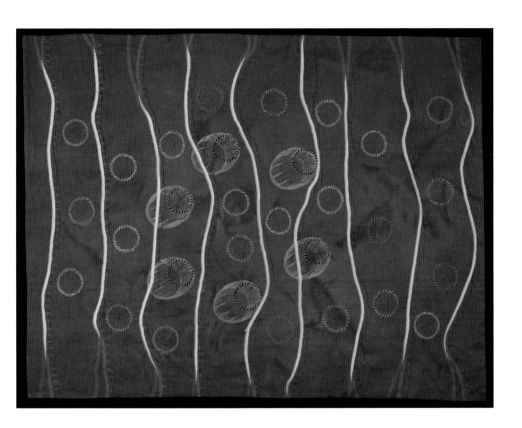

Fig. 60. *Tunicata VI: Inner Circle*, 2019. 30 × 39.5 in.

Fig. 61. *Midnight Garden #1*, 2019. 10 × 10 in. (framed).

Fig. 62. *Midnight Garden #2*, 2019. 10 × 10 in. (framed).

Fig. 63. *Midnight Garden #3*, 2019. 10 × 10 in. (framed).

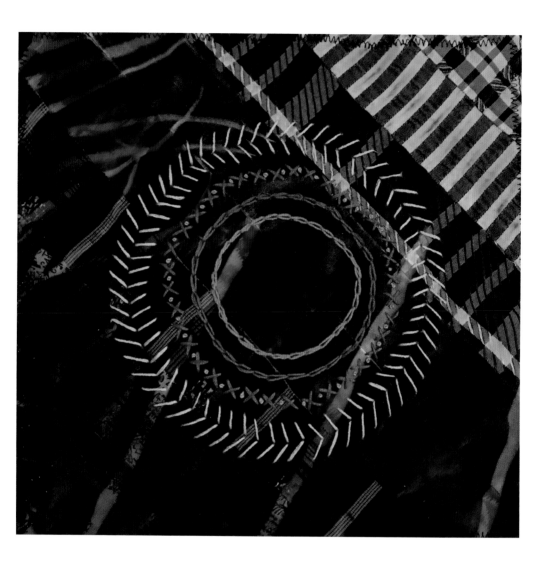

Fig. 64. *Midnight Garden #4*, 2019. 10 × 10 in. (framed).

Fig. 65. *Midnight Garden #5*, 2019. 10 × 10 in. (framed).